DARE TO PAIR

THE ULTIMATE GUIDE TO

CHOCOLATE AND WINE PAIRING

Another delicious book by Julie Pech

Adapted from the author's book, *The Chocolate Therapist: A User's Guide to the Extraordinary Health Benefits of Chocolate*

Printed in the United States of America

ISBN-13: 978-1500141899
ISBN-10: 1500141895

For Britt and Blake. My life is
so much sweeter because you're in it.

CONTENTS

ACKNOWLEDGMENTS

Thank you to the thousands of you who have attended my classes and have been the guinea-pigs, testing wine after wine, chocolate after chocolate—it was a lot of work, but you hung in there. Thank you Erik & Rebekah, who helped bring the pairing process to a whole new level. Thank you to my extraordinary staff at The Chocolate Therapist and to Erin, for managing the shop so I could finish this book. Thank you Mary Carol, chocolatier-extraordinaire. And thank you Maryann, my brilliant and peaceful graphic artist, who really did everything else.

We've toasted abroad, we've toasted at home,
The chocolate enticing, never alone.

And along the journey, we discovered THE rule,
The precious secret of "Wine Pairing School"

If you ever discover a marginal pair,
Just keep drinking, my friend
And soon you won't care.

1 How It All Got Started

I know what you're thinking: chocolate and wine pairing is an interesting concept to say the least. When I first heard about it over a decade ago, my initial reaction was "why?" followed shortly after by "why not?" Fortunately, the job of learning about it came into my life out of sheer necessity. The work started shortly after the release of my book *The Chocolate Therapist*. A series of serendipitous events led to an opportunity to travel on cruise ships, giving lectures about chocolate. In the process of booking the first cruise, I was asked for the titles of *all* my lectures to confirm my reservation. This request surprised me because I'd only planned on lecturing about the health benefits of chocolate. But cruise ship policy calls for a series of lectures on the same topic, not the same topic five times. (I thought I'd share this fact with you in case you're thinking about presenting a topic.)

To keep things simple and fun, I quickly came up with a series of lectures: "Chocolate and Wine Pairing," "Chocolate and Tea Pairing," "International Chocolates," "How to Throw a Chocolate Party," and, my original lecture, "The Extraordinary Health Benefits of Chocolate." I sent the list and secured my spot, a little later realizing that the only topic I knew anything about was the health benefits of chocolate. But I decided not to let a complete lack of knowing what I was doing stand in the way. Cruising to

Bermuda and the Eastern Caribbean was on the line, so I'd have to figure it out.

I needed some practice fast. A bottle of wine and a box of chocolates seemed like a good place to start, and as I was polishing off my fourth pairing, it occurred to me that I might fare better doing the research with a group. If I did everything myself, it seemed unlikely that I'd fit into any of my clothes by the time the cruise date arrived. I also wanted to keep on track with the principle I was teaching in my lecture on the health benefits of chocolate: to be healthy, a person should eat between one and two ounces of good-quality dark chocolate a day at the most. This meant discovering a plan that didn't include a half pound of chocolate and a couple of glasses of wine a day (although the idea didn't seem half bad). I presented my idea for a chocolate- and wine-pairing class to Colorado Free University, a local continuing education facility. They loved the concept, and shortly thereafter I began teaching the classes, my experience limited to anything I could find in books (not much) and my own short-list of pairings.

The first classes were rather humorous—the perfect example of learning on the job. Although I'd researched every fact I could find about chocolate and wine pairing, putting it into a presentation didn't come naturally to me. I cut all the information into little pieces and meticulously reviewed every item with the class. It took hours to prepare for each class, and it was confusing for the students as they sifted through their folders, trying to find my notes on the chocolate or wine we were discussing. I also poured the wine much too early, a strategy that in hindsight proved to be completely counterproductive. From the first sip, it was almost impossible to recapture anyone's attention. (I've since adopted a strict policy: education first, *then* drinking.) The classes were too long, and they contained too much information. And then there were the pairings, often frightful, as I used my early students as the unfortunate guinea pigs. (Note to self: Muscato should always be served chilled.) Fortunately, we learned one of the cardinal rules of pairing early on: If you don't like a combination, just keep drinking! Eventually everything pairs perfectly.

I kept teaching and learning, adjusting and sharing, taking notes and revamping. Slowly I was learning how to pair chocolate and wine. In the meantime having my class listed in Colorado Free University's catalog came with an unexpected benefit. The university sent the catalog out to over thirty thousand people per quarter, and I soon found myself being asked to host corporate chocolate and wine events and private parties. People assumed that if I was teaching a class on the subject, I must know what I'm doing. I decided to bear the burden of my new "chocolate and wine pairing expert" title. I figured since the topic was so new, it was certain that I knew more about chocolate and wine pairing than most people anyway.

Somewhere during the early classes, I took my first cruise. The year was 2006. The cruise company asked me to prepare for about twenty to thirty guests, the average attendance for an enrichment lecturer. I considered this request and instead prepared for fifty guests. I was giving away free chocolate, after all, something that has probably never occurred on a cruise ship. It seemed likely that more than twenty people would show up. It was an eight-day cruise, and I had been asked to prepare four lectures. It seemed easy enough, but during the preparation I also had to discover the art of packing enough information for fifty people to attend four classes, while keeping the total weight of the materials under fifty pounds (to avoid the airline's heavy-bag fee). After repacking a mere seven times, I discovered that it *is* possible.

True to my estimate, I had excellent attendance for every class. On the day of the chocolate- and wine-pairing class, the room was filled with guests. Free wine and chocolate on a cruise ship? Who *wasn't* there? With that many guests attending, the wine samples were so small they were barely recognizable, but people still loved the class. The cruise director was thrilled with the turnout. It helped, of course, that on my arrival I'd given her a signed book and a collection of chocolates to keep things moving smoothly. (Note: this is an excellent strategy for all speakers, even if you're not in the chocolate business.) Guests stayed long after the class was over and bought all of my books, even though that first edition of the book didn't include a chapter on chocolate and wine pairing. For the next five years, I took one to three cruises a year, traveling all over the world, teaching people about chocolate. I suppose someone had to do it.

Between cruises I spoke about chocolate's health benefits to any group that would listen. The first two years I spoke for free, surviving on after-event book sales and my fees from chocolate- and wine-pairing events. When demand exceeded my available time, I started to charge for the presentations, and things barely slowed down. (Note to self: I probably should have done that a little sooner.) Chocolate companies sponsored me in the beginning, but at some point I had my "aha" moment and decided to start my own brand. I developed a small line of chocolate bars to sell with the book while I was out speaking and hired a local company to manufacture the bars. Book sales doubled as soon as I had my own line, prompting another "I probably should have done that sooner" moment. It's true that we only know exactly what to do in hindsight.

Everything was going great! I was selling thousands of books and chocolate bars, speaking regularly, and having lots of fun. The company making my bars was doing all the work. It seemed like a perfect arrangement to me. They must have gotten wise to the situation because right about this time, the owners decided to retire. My available choices: buy the shop or find a commercial kitchen. Having worked in retail when I was younger, I knew that buying a retail shop would be like having triplets—don't plan on going anywhere any time soon. It would be in direct contrast to my free-spirited entrepreneurial style.

Nonetheless, after thinking it through, I realized that I didn't want to manage production in a commercial kitchen. After a few negotiations, I found myself the proud owner of a chocolate shop. Other than writing the book, my only experience in chocolate production was limited to a passion for making homemade chocolate-chip oatmeal cookies. I now owned a chocolate shop without a single brain cell of working knowledge about how to make chocolate. Was it going to be enough?

I include this story about purchasing the shop because it proves that you don't really have to know as much as you think you do to make something work. Occasionally I give empowerment presentations to entrepreneurs, and I always encourage people to skip the step that's stopping them and figure it out later. Now I had to walk my own talk. Although I had extensive knowledge of nutrition when I wrote *The Chocolate Therapist*, I didn't know anything about chocolate, and things had been working out just fine with that. I asked myself, "How can this be any different?" Blind optimism is the perfect cliché simply because it works. All

4

I really needed was passion and purpose, and I had plenty of that.

The main chocolatier had stayed on after the purchase, which was quite helpful since I had no idea how to make chocolate. But just a month later, the person who had originally started the business twenty years earlier asked to come back and work at the shop, an unexpected stroke of good fortune because she was (and still is) an extraordinary chocolatier.

One of the first things I decided to do was to change all the recipes. The goal was to create products free from dyes, preservatives, or artificial ingredients of any kind, and to make chocolate that supported the pure eating concepts in *The Chocolate Therapist*. This is the way I try to eat (to the extent that it's possible in today's world), and that's what *The Chocolate Therapist* is all about. It was important that everything we created in the shop reflect this message. The chocolatier and I went through the recipes, making changes and figuring out a way to create new products with all-natural ingredients.

People were a little surprised when we changed the recipes, especially considering I had no experience making chocolate. Many people told me it was a bad decision and that I'd lose customers (entrepreneur tip: when other people think it's a bad idea, you're usually on the right track). And I couldn't be out there speaking about all-natural eating, then sending people to my shop to buy chocolate made with dyes and artificial flavors.

Up until that point, I'd been using other brands for my chocolate- and wine-pairing events, but once we developed a clean ingredient line, I started using our new chocolates. I noticed right away how the pairings improved: pure chocolate and organic flavoring oils were far better than the mysterious ingredients of the other brands I'd been serving. We put all of our focus into creating clean chocolates and started overhauling the entire Chocolate Therapist line.

I'd owned the shop for about eighteen months when business really started picking up. I hired an additional chocolatier who turned out to be a wine enthusiast. She and I started sampling wines and eating chocolate on a regular basis (it was tough). We stepped up the inventing process and tested out new chocolate concoctions with various wines. A year later, we enlisted the services of Groupon, a national online coupon and promotions company to help sell chocolate and wine pairing classes at the shop. We sold out every class for months. My wine-loving chocolatier learned how to teach the classes so that we could keep up with the demand. Looking back, I don't recall ever dreading going to work.

To get the information out to as many people as possible, *Dare to Pair* became a necessary part of the process. Every event we hosted was always a great success, and each experience was unique. We discovered there was no terrible pairing because every palate is different: one person's miss is another person's perfect pairing (but skip the lemon dark chocolate with a red zinfandel to be sure). Fortunately, if you don't like the pairing, you still end up with a little chocolate and a little wine—just don't put them in your mouth at the same time!

It helps to have some basic strategies and ideas to start with when creating the optimal pairing experience. Nine years of research is presented in *Dare to Pair*. Some of you will be tempted to zip right to the pairings; but without at least a small working knowledge of chocolate and wine pairing, there might be some confusion as to how to proceed. Personally, I think it's important to understand all the basics, so it's better to start at the beginning of the book and move on from there. Take a moment to skim the next sections if you're prone to leap ahead. You can always come back if you need a few more answers.

2 Chocolate and Wine Basics

News Breaks on Wine and Health

The news about red wine and heart health first came out in 1991 on *60 Minutes*. The phenomenon was called the French paradox, and the show focused on the fact that the French, who drink considerably more wine than Americans, have much lower levels of heart disease. The story ran twice that year, and Americans responded by increasing their purchases of red wine the following year by nearly 40 percent. *This* is how we embrace a health trend.

Similar information is now being released about chocolate. Although we don't see medical professionals encouraging us to eat chocolate every day, some doctors and dieticians are suggesting an ounce per day for health. As more research reveals the health benefits of dark chocolate, we're likely to see even more positive support.

Similarities between Chocolate and Wine

Chocolate and wine share many of the same qualities when it comes to pairing and tasting, the first being that both are fruits. We've known this about wine for centuries, but many people don't realize that chocolate is also made from a fruit.

The processing of chocolate and wine is also very similar. Cocoa processing involves harvesting the pods, splitting the pods and scooping out the beans, fermenting and roasting the beans, winnowing the nibs, and finally grinding the nibs into a thick chocolate soup called chocolate liquor—the basis of all things chocolate.

Wine starts with the harvest, followed by crushing the grapes, fermenting, blending (depending on the wine being produced), aging, and bottling the finished product. Both chocolate and wine are rich in antioxidants because both are made from the ground seeds of a fruit tree. One could argue that producing chocolate is a bit more labor intensive than making wine, but many elements are the same.

More similarities between the two are found in their growing regions. Both grapes and cacao come from regions all over the world. Cacao requires a hot, humid environment and grows in a band approximately ten degrees north and south of the equator. Grapes grow twenty to sixty degrees north and south of the equator, just outside the band of the cacao growing region. Because of this, grapes grow in an estimated sixty countries, whereas only thirty-three countries currently grow cacao.

Within various countries, cacao tree types change from region to region, and the taste of the beans also changes—just as grapes do. The trees pick up the nuances of the land and pass its flavors into the cacao beans. The same characteristics are found in grape vines as well. There are hundreds flavor compounds in both wine and chocolate, making the possible combinations unlimited, so you better get started.

3 Proper Chocolate Consumption

Eating chocolate properly is an important step in appreciating a good pairing. In fact when people come into our shop after having taken the chocolate and wine pairing class, the idea they mention the most is how much they appreciated this part of the class. In general, people eat far too fast, so the intent of this section is to learn how to slow down. There's simply no way to discover the many flavor compounds of chocolate if it's in and out of your mouth in less than ten seconds. Food should arrive in your stomach in liquid form. How often does that actually happen?

This section requires your own personal flavor research. If you don't already have a piece of chocolate nearby, time to head toward the chocolate stash now (you know you have one). At the very least, sneak into the pantry for a handful of chocolate chips. Learning how to eat chocolate properly isn't that complicated and is well worth the effort.

There's a good chance you've never considered whether you eat chocolate properly. I'd been a devout consumer for decades, and the thought never entered my mind. I was amused to discover that there are actually published guidelines to assist with just such a task, as if we truly needed help. Once I read them, I discovered I'd been doing it wrong all along. Fortunately, having an imperfect technique didn't appear to affect my love for chocolate. Yet once I learned how to indulge correctly, it made all the difference. Even if you have your own technique perfected, take a moment to review this section to make sure you're getting all the critical steps.

First of all, chocolate tastes best when eaten on an empty stomach. In the event that you find yourself with an empty stomach, this could be the perfect time for a chocolate tasting. I noticed the guidelines failed to mention what would happen if you *didn't* have an empty stomach. After some personal research, I concluded that regardless of the condition of your stomach, chocolate can be eaten without any negative side effects. (Although if you have ulcers, do not eat chocolate on an empty stomach because it has been reported to occasionally aggravate this condition.)

Now you're ready to begin the actual tasting. Pick up the chocolate and observe it as you would a work of fine art, taking time to examine its beauty and perfection. This step should last anywhere from five to twenty seconds. Since chocolate melts at 94°F, or slightly below body temperature, holding the chocolate starts the melting process, which helps release its aromas into the air. Gently wave the chocolate before your nose as you inhale the many tantalizing aromas. Ninety percent of everything you taste comes from your sense of smell, so if you skip this step, you miss a considerable part of the experience.

Slowly place the chocolate in your mouth, allowing your lips to sense the gentle softness of the chocolate's texture. Let it sit in your mouth for a few seconds and begin melting on your tongue. As you start to chew, swirl the chocolate around your mouth.

The idea is to allow the entire mouth to experience the chocolate. Some research claims that the tongue has four zones: salt, sour, bitter, and sweet. Yet more recent research suggests that the entire tongue tastes most flavors and that there are taste buds on the soft palate and upper epiglottis as well. Why take chances, though? Swirl it around for your own benefit, zones or no zones. Chocolate has hundreds of flavor compounds, and once you slow down and focus, you'll start to notice more of them.

Continue chewing as you swirl, but don't swallow just yet. Take a moment to press the chocolate onto the roof of your mouth with your tongue, savoring one last moment of melting and flavor euphoria. Relax, breathe deeply, and take in the lingering cacophony of sensations. Once you've completed this final step of delicious enjoyment, swallow at last. Note the flavors as they fade away: you may find something different that you didn't taste while it was in your mouth.

If you're sampling another type of chocolate, rinse your mouth thoroughly with water, light tea, or wine to prepare the palate for the next unique experience. Some connoisseurs insist on rinsing with water only because wine or tea can desensitize taste buds. Yet others recommend consuming chocolate with wine, which, of course, is what this book is all about. It seems like a personal preference to me—of course you should do exactly what you want. Fortunately, every choice wins because chocolate is involved in all cases.

The best way to learn about bean flavors is to sample single origin chocolates, meaning all of the cocoa beans that make up the bar have come from a single country. Since the beans pick up the nuances of the land where they're grown, different countries have very different flavor profiles. Once you've acquired the skills of an advanced connoisseur, you'll be able to discern a wide variety of bean flavors without even referring to the wrapper. Be prepared for an entertaining variety of subtle flavor sensations, such as spices, pepper, mango, pineapple, raspberry, cream, espresso, blueberry, lavender, almond, coffee, and even tobacco.

It's easier to identify flavors when you have them listed in front of you. To help train your palate, the "Blommer's Chocolate Wheel of Flavor," developed by Rose Potts of Blommer Chocolate Company, is included here. Once a piece of chocolate has thoroughly melted in your mouth, check the flavor wheel to help you uncover the mysteries. It seems obvious that you would know what you're tasting, but sometimes you won't remember a flavor until you see its name. With the wheel, you'll have dozens of choices in front of you.

The good news is that even if you've been eating chocolate incorrectly for years, no harm will come of it. My previous method involved directly placing the chocolate into my mouth (although not slowly, as advised), quickly chewing and then going straight for the next confection. The discovery of all the missing steps was a delightful surprise. Luckily, it's never too late to change. Once you've started making step-by-step adjustments, you may realize some of those steps are rather valuable. Pass the wine, please.

Blommer Chocolate Flavor/Aroma Wheel

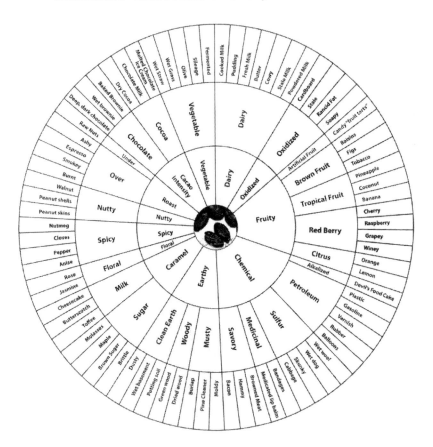

Use this chart to learn all the flavors of chocolate to become a discerning connoisseur.

The Chocolate Flavor/Aroma Wheel was developed by Rose Potts or Blommer's Chocolate Company. Permission granted to use this image by Blommer Chocolate Company. (Blommer Chocolate Company: East Greenville, Pennsylvania; Chicago, Illinois; Union City, California; Campbellford, Ontario.) For your own copy of this copyrighted flavor wheel, contact Blommer through their website at www.blommer.com.

4 Selecting the Proper Wine Glass

The next step is a brief review on how to enjoy wine from the correct glass. It's not imperative to have the precise glass, of course, but knowing the best choice gives you an option if you want to use it.

Anyone who has dined in the twenty-first century has undoubtedly noticed that various wines are served in different-shaped glasses. Entire classes are devoted to the topic, but to keep things simple, the following information is a condensed version of everything you need to know.

White-wine glass: This glass is typically smaller than a red-wine glass to concentrate the bouquet (or smell) in the glass. Make sure to breathe in the aromas before you sip to appreciate the wine from this glass. The glass is also slightly closed at the top to help maintain the temperature of the wine, which is primarily served chilled.

Red-wine glass: This larger, balloon-shaped glass helps oxidize the wine once it's out of the bottle, adding flavor and bouquet to the overall experience. Swirling the wine in the glass helps release the aromas. Take care not to get too overzealous in your churning or you may end up dousing your date with wine (however, this is an excellent strategy if you want to leave early).

Champagne glass: The long, fluted shape of this glass serves two purposes: it helps keep the Champagne cool and also releases the bubbles from a single point, preserving the Champagne just a bit longer. Also, if you take care not to chug it, bubble watching can offer stimulating entertainment at a boring dinner party.

Port glass: The primary reason for the smaller size of this glass is to allow you to enjoy a full glass while drinking a smaller amount of port. The unusual expense of port makes the smaller glass a good concept for dining establishments but not such a good value for the consumer. On a positive note, considering the higher alcohol content of port along with the likelihood that you'll be drinking it closer to the end of the evening, the smaller glass also serves as protection against the possibility of overindulging.

How to Taste Wine

Just like chocolate, there are published guidelines on how to taste wine properly. If you're like most people, you've been drinking wine without much consideration for years, but change is good and the time is now.

Ideally, your wine should be poured into the proper glass for maximum flavor and aroma. In case you skipped that section, it's right before this one and takes less than two minutes to read.

Red wine should be opened before you serve it to help aerate the wine, although not much happens in that regard unless it's poured into a decanter. To really release the aromas and aerate red wine, pour it into a larger container. White wine is normally served chilled and occasionally at room temperature.

Next pour the wine into the glass and observe the color. Some people prefer to hold a white cloth or napkin to the back of the glass to get a true assessment of color. Deeper colors are generally associated with more intense flavors.

Swirl the wine in the glass to help release its aroma and nuances. While it runs back down the side of the glass, note the viscosity. If you see the wine running down the glass, it's said to have "legs." Take a long sniff or two to stimulate your olfactory glands and help wake up your taste buds. As mentioned in the chocolate tasting chapter, smell is accountable for as much as ninety percent of everything you taste, so it's in your best interest to take time for this step.

Next take a small sip of the wine, but don't swallow immediately. Keep it in your mouth and swirl it around your tongue, looking for flavor notes such as fruit, oak, earth, mineral, sweet, sour, bitter, and salty. Observe the texture—is it smooth, light, full, or delicate?

Try taking a breath though your nose with the wine still in your mouth. Think carefully about this procedure, as taking a breath while swallowing could cause some problems. The key, of course, is not to swallow exactly at the same time you're breathing.

The last step, finally, is to swallow. But your job isn't finished! How long does the flavor last? What are the lingering nuances? Is it sweet, acidic, robust, tannic, or strong in alcohol? There are so many things to consider. You may have to take another sip or two to get it right.

To help with flavor identification, see the "Wine Aroma Wheel" by Ann Noble on the next page. Having the flavors at your fingertips can help you determine a wine's exact essences and aromas. The strategy here is the same as the "Blommer Chocolate Wheel of Flavor." Once you have the wine in your mouth, look at the different flavors on the wheel to help you discern what you are tasting.

The Wine Aroma Wheel

This is an excellent reference for discovering and learning
the flavors in wines.

Putting It All Together

People always ask me what they should put in their mouth first when pairing—the wine or the chocolate? Personally, I prefer to put the chocolate in my mouth first, taking special care to follow the proper chocolate consumption instructions. This gives the chocolate a chance to melt before you add the wine. If the wine is cool and you drink it before eating the chocolate, it can lower the temperature of your mouth and make the melting process more challenging.

As you're assessing the chocolate, pour about a third of a glass of wine. Swirl the wine in the glass and take short sniffs, as reviewed in "How to Taste Wine." Take a small sip and swish the wine around with the chocolate so the two mingle together. Note how the flavors of the chocolate have changed. Some of the flavors will be accentuated by the wine; others will be covered up. Sometimes the wine is too strong for the chocolate, or the chocolate may be too strong for the wine. You're looking for balance. The perfect pairing accentuates both the wine and the chocolate.

After you've paired the wine and chocolate in this order, you may want to reverse the process and drink the wine first, followed by eating the chocolate. Remember to go slowly: smell the wine, take a small sip, and note the flavors, then add the chocolate and note how the flavors of both the chocolate and the wine change. If you rush, this takes away from the process, and you'll miss quite a few of the flavors. Remember, there are hundreds of flavors between the chocolate and the wine!

Before you switch to the next pairing, cleanse your palate with bland crackers or water. A salt-free table cracker works well because the goal of a palate cleanser is to neutralize the palate. I prefer to stay away from salt because it changes the palate considerably, and it changes the flavor of chocolate as well. If you're using water, it's best to drink it without ice to avoid cooling your mouth.

5 Red Wine and
Chocolate Pairings

For pairing purposes it's important to note that wines are generally classified into three different body types: light, medium, and full. A light-bodied wine is in and out of your mouth quickly, and you taste it only while it's in your mouth. It's also typically lighter in color, and you can see through it. Lighter reds generally have higher acidity levels and are best drunk when relatively young. Open a bottle of light-bodied red wine, and you'll want to finish the bottle immediately. Examples of lighter reds include pinot noir, gamay, Beaujolais, and an occasional merlot.

A medium-bodied wine lingers awhile once you've swallowed it, allowing you to assess the taste and aftertaste longer than the lighter wines. It's generally a moderate shade of red or burgundy. It contains more tannins than the lighter reds, although you'll still want to enjoy this wine right after opening the bottle. Leave it around longer than four days, and most of the flavor will be gone. To stretch out its life, put it in the refrigerator to help keep it from oxidizing. Examples of medium-bodied wines include merlot, Sangiovese, and occasionally zinfandel, although these wines can be full-bodied as well.

Full-bodied wine flavors last long after the wine has been swallowed and offer changing taste sensations on the finish. The color is deep and rich—not something that can easily be gazed through. The fullest wines also have the highest level of tannins. Full-bodied wines last a little longer as well. After two days, you may discover flavors you didn't notice on opening. Examples of full-bodied wines include cabernet sauvignon, cabernet franc, and Shiraz.

The details provided for each wine in the pairing section that follows are general, and you won't taste every flavor listed for each wine. Flavors depend on many elements, such as growing regions, production techniques, the average temperature during the growing season, and more. The following are flavors you *may* find in each wine. They're included here because having a list will help you discern flavors you might not otherwise be able to identify. It will also help you pair the chocolates more appropriately.

All recipes identified by an asterisk (*) can be found in the back of this book.

AMARONE

Grapes used to make: Corvina, Rondinella, Sangiovese, Molinara

Regions grown in: Italy/Veneto

Body: Full bodied, soft tannins, higher alcohol, often dry, long flavor

Flavors: Dried fruit, ripe wild berries, candied fruit, chocolate, charcoal, cinnamon, baked cherries, smoke, truffle, port, earth

Notes: Whatever you're serving, make sure it's powerful enough to withstand the strength of this popular Italian wine. It's a great wine for foods with bold tastes and particularly nice with a cheese plate. Try a dark chocolate mole' sauce with fresh raspberries over chicken.

Adventurous Chocolate Pairings

- 🍇 Conservative: Dark chocolate cherry truffle
- 🍇 Edgy: 70 percent melted dark chocolate, dried blueberries, and vanilla.
- 🍇 Gone Wild: Raspberry Truffle Brownies* with a Raspberry/Pomegranate Purée*

🍷 BARBARESCO 🍷

Grapes used to make: Nebbiolo

Regions grown in: Italy/Piedmont, California

Body: Medium to full bodied, bold, spicy, tannic, elegant, good balance, long on palate; a powerful wine that holds up well with bold flavors

Flavors: Earth, fig, nut, leather, tar, mushroom, vanilla, cinnamon, plum, raspberry, black cherry, violet, truffle, rose, sweet red fruit, licorice, menthol, mineral, spice

Notes: The hallmark flavors of Barbaresco are tar and roses, so better to focus on bringing up the rose than the tar. Try Vosges's Le Chocolat en Rose Truffles: a twenty-piece truffle collection, for an evening of dedicated decadence (www.VosgesChocolate.com).

Adventurous Chocolate Pairings

- 🍇 Conservative: Single-origin Ecuadorian chocolate, known for its anise flavor
- 🍇 Edgy: Dark rose truffles, as mentioned above
- 🍇 Gone Wild: Dark chocolate infused with black cherry oil

🍷 BARBERA 🍷

Grapes used to make: Nebbiolo

Regions grown in: Italy/Piedmont, California

Body: Medium bodied, smooth, low tannins with high acidity

Flavors: Blackberry, black cherry, plum, black pepper, cinnamon, vanilla, smoke, milk chocolate, cedar, toasted oak, mineral, chocolate, spice, raspberry, earth

Notes: This wine is particularly suited to Mediterranean foods, making it ideal for pairing with fruits from the same region, such as red currants, cranberries, and gooseberries.

Adventurous Chocolate Pairings

- **Conservative: Milk and dark chocolate together, melted and lightly swirled with a sprinkle of dried pomegranate seeds**
- **Edgy: Dark chocolate with chili**
- **Gone Wild: Double Dark Chocolate Brownies* topped with fresh blackberries, raspberries and melted dark chocolate**

BAROLO

Grapes used to make: Nebbiolo

Regions grown in: Italy/Piedmont, California

Body: Medium to full bodied, rich, heavy, high alcohol content, higher tannins when young

Flavors: Black cherry, leather, tar, earth, mushroom, chocolate, flowers, rose, herbs, wood, hazelnut, berries, coconut, vanilla, raspberry, spice, oregano, tobacco, anise, smoke, violet

Notes: Salt has a tendency to make tannic wines slightly sweeter, hence the edgy recommendation for a bit of sea salt with the pairing. Who better than you to determine whether this adventure is one worth repeating?

Adventurous Chocolate Pairings

- **Conservative: Dark chocolate raspberry (try Chocolove's dark chocolate raspberry bar, www.Chocolove.com)**
- **Edgy: Chocolate mousse with a hint of sea salt**

🍫 Gone Wild: Dried mangos dipped in 70% single-origin Sao Thome chocolate with a drop of vanilla melted in.

🍷 BEAUJOLAIS 🍷

Grapes used to make: Gamay

Regions grown in: France/Burgundy region of Beaujolais, Switzerland

Body: Light body, low tannins, refreshing

Flavors: Berries, cherry, blackberry, strawberry, black currant, cedar, earth, leather, flowers

Beaujolais: Made from 100 percent gamay grapes, generally light and fruity

Beaujolais Nouveau: The lightest, fruitiest, and youngest of the Beaujolais family. The time from harvest to retail is often less than two months. Once you open the bottle, consume it within hours or there will hardly be anything left to taste.

Beaujolais Villages: A step up from Nouveau, Beaujolais Villages wines are produced in regions known to produce higher-quality grapes.

Beaujolais Cru: The best Beaujolais money can buy. Look for the word *cru* on the label.

Notes: When considering chocolate, go for the lighter dark chocolate, such as 45 to 55 percent dark with fruity and/or nutty nuances. Very dark chocolate will bury the wine, and you'll end up with bitterness. Also note that citrus and cream flavors can clash with Beaujolais.

Adventurous Chocolate Pairings

🍫 Conservative: Milk chocolate with dried currants
🍫 Edgy: Melted 55 percent dark chocolate with dried cherries and a drop or two of vanilla
🍫 Gone Wild: Sliced red apples dipped in a blend of melted cheddar cheese and 50 percent dark chocolate

🍷 BORDEAUX 🍷

Grapes used to make: Usually a combination of cabernet sauvignon, merlot, cabernet franc, Malbec, and Petit Verdot.

Regions grown in: France/Bordeaux, Italy

Body: Medium to full bodied, soft to moderate tannins, smooth

Flavors: Oak, blackberry, Indian spices, licorice, green olive, dark olive, plum, mineral, flowers, jam, cherry, strawberry, smoke, earth, cassis, black currant, dried herbs, toast, herb, vanilla, cedar, roasted coffee, mocha, cola

<u>Notes</u>: Bordeaux is any wine produced in the Bordeaux region of France, so narrowing the field of flavors and grapes is almost impossible. Read the labels to determine the flavors of your Bordeaux, and then select the chocolate accordingly.

Adventurous Chocolate Pairings

- 🍫 **Conservative: Dark chocolate with dried blueberries**
- 🍫 **Edgy: Melt milk or dark chocolate, stir in dried cherries and a sprinkle of cinnamon, pour thin onto wax paper, refrigerate, break into bark, and serve**
- 🍫 **Gone Wild: Dark chocolate with fresh ground espresso (try the Double Shot bar, available at www.TheChocolateTherapist.com)**

🍷 BRUNELLO 🍷

Grapes used to make: Brunello, Sangiovese

Regions grown in: Italy/Tuscany

Body: Full bodied, generally longer on finish, strength in tannins

Flavors: Blackberry, vanilla, Indian spices, currant, toasted oak, cherry, berry, anise, menthol, cedar, earth, tea, raspberry, smoke, chocolate truffles, black mushroom, blueberry, plums, prunes, tar, chestnuts

Notes: Brunello is the signature wine of Italy's Montalcino region, considered by some to be one of Italy's best wines. Unexpected bold flavors and aromas keep the chocolate pairing options wide open for negotiation, so if you don't see something that piques your palate here, investigate a collection of your own concoctions.

Adventurous Chocolate Pairings

- Conservative: **Raspberry Dark Chocolate Truffles***
- Edgy: **Chili pepper patties (TheChocolateTherapist.com)**
- Gone Wild: **Melt dark chocolate, stir in hazelnuts and a pinch of nutmeg, spread onto wax paper and cool in refrigerator, break into bark.**

BURGUNDY

Grapes used to make: Pinot noir, less expensive wines may also include gamay

Regions grown in: France/Burgundy

Body: Medium to full bodied; full, ripe tannins; long finish

Flavors: Raspberry, plum, spice, flowers, blackberry, cherry, leather, earth, pomegranate, vanilla, chocolate, apple, pineapple, banana, mayflower, hazelnut

Notes: The Burgundy region in France produces both red and white wines. A true red Burgundy is made only from the pinot noir grape, although less expensive versions may include gamay grapes as well. Blends are considered second class to the great Burgundies of the region.

Adventurous Chocolate Pairings

- Conservative: **Dark chocolate with organic plum oil (available at www.TheChocolateTherapist.com, Pairing Chocolates)**

- Edgy: **Pomegranate and Cinnamon Double Dark Chocolate Brownies**
- Gone Wild: **Dark chocolate cake with melted chocolate drizzle**

CABERNET FRANC

Grapes used to make: Cabernet franc, cabernet sauvignon, merlot

Regions grown in: France/Bordeaux and Loire Valley, California/Napa Valley, Washington State

Body: Medium to full bodied, gentle tannins, high acidity

Flavors: Red berries, plum, cinnamon, tea, cedar, spice, green peppers, cocoa powder, savory, flowers, tarragon, dried cherry, coffee, anise, herbs, white pepper, vanilla, tobacco leaf, allspice, clove, toffee, cream, raspberry, currant, blackberry, mineral

Notes: Cabernet franc is generally blended with the two grapes mentioned above, although it's possible to find wine made from cabernet franc grapes alone. This versatile wine often contains chocolate notes on the finish, making it a natural for pairing.

Adventurous Chocolate Pairings

- Conservative: **Dark chocolate flourless torte with fresh raspberries and blackberries**
- Edgy: **Chocolate pudding cups sprinkled with cocoa nibs**
- Gone Wild: **Chocolate Kahlua Truffles***

CABERNET SAUVIGNON

Grapes used to make: Cabernet sauvignon (at least 75 percent), merlot, Shiraz

Regions grown in: France/Bordeaux, California (mostly dry cabs),

Australia (always dry), Chile, Argentina, Italy, Spain, Washington State

Body: Full bodied, robust, hearty, big tannins, acidic, deeply colored, concentrated flavors, dense, structured

Flavors: Dark chocolate, black currant, tobacco, blackberry, plum, cherry, mint, green pepper, bitter, woody, vanilla, earth, Havana leaf, espresso, licorice, blueberry, violet, eucalyptus, spice, truffles, leather, toasty oak

Notes: For centuries, cabernet sauvignon reigned as the world's most planted premium grape, an arguable statement as some sources claim it's the Grenache grape. Drop back to 2005 and most sites report merlot as number one. Regardless of its status, the cabernet grape's thick skins make for a bold, tannic, and widely flavorful wine. It can be quite an adventure to pair this powerful wine with chocolate (an opinion, of course).

Adventurous Chocolate Pairings

- **Conservative: 72 percent dark chocolate with cacao nibs sprinkled on top**
- **Edgy: Chocolate-Chip Oatmeal Cookies* dipped in melted dark chocolate**
- **Gone Wild: Milk or dark chocolate mint meltaways (available at www.TheChocolateTherapist.com)**

♟ CHIANTI ♟

Grapes used to make: Sangiovese (80 percent), cabernet sauvignon, merlot, Syrah

Regions grown in: Italy/Tuscany, California/Napa Valley

Body: Light to medium bodied, bright acidity, higher in tannins, tannic finish

Flavors: Cherry, bay leaf, coffee, apple, leather, herb, earth, chocolate, intense dark fruit, citrus in the nose, vanilla, licorice (finish), red plum, cedar, violet, raspberry, toasty oak

Notes: This Italian wine pairs perfectly with Italian entrées like seasoned meats, pizza, sausage, and pasta. This makes it easy to venture out with an Italian-themed dessert like chocolate tiramisu, double chocolate hazelnut biscotti, or even a chocolate tortoni.

Adventurous Chocolate Pairings

- Conservative: 65 percent single-origin dark chocolate from Madagascar
- Edgy: Chocolate tiramisu
- Gone Wild: Shortbread cookies dipped in melted dark chocolate, sprinkled with cinnamon

DOLCETTO

Grapes used to make: Dolcetto

Regions grown in: Italy/Piedmont, Australia, California (where the grapes are called douce noire)

Body: Light to medium bodied, easy to drink, low acid

Flavors: Black cherry, licorice, almond, prune, fruit, jam

Notes: *Dolcetto* translates to "little sweet one," but don't look for a little, sweet wine here. While the name implies "wine cuteness," expect a little tannic snap on the back end from this Italian black grape. Choose a lower percentage chocolate to avoid overpowering the wine.

Adventurous Chocolate Pairings

- Conservative: Chocolate-covered dried Bing cherries
- Edgy: Melted dark chocolate with cranberries and a sprinkle of nutmeg
- Gone Wild: Dark Chocolate Cake with Chocolate/Apricot Sauce and sliced almonds

GRENACHE

Grapes used to make: Grenache

Regions grown in: France, Spain, Italy, California, Australia

Body: Medium to full bodied

Flavors: Raisin, currant, spice, blackberry, raspberry, cherry, blueberry, cinnamon, strawberry, vanilla

Notes: Grenache is to France as Garnacha is to Spain: both produce wines that are made from the same grape and work wonderfully with chocolate. Look for a full-bodied selection of this often fruit-forward wine, and choose international brands for excellent quality.

Adventurous Chocolate Pairings

- **Conservative: Dark chocolate-covered strawberries**
- **Edgy: Cayenne Pepper Savouries (available at www.TheChocolateTherapist.com)**
- **Gone Wild: Brownies with tart dried cherries**

MALBEC

Grapes used to make: Malbec, cabernet sauvignon, occasionally Tannat

Regions grown in: Argentina, France/Bordeaux

Body: Full, refreshing acidity, sweet tannins

Flavors: Black fruit, flowers, leather, vanilla, spice, black raspberry, black cherry, violet, black pepper, anise, smoke, currant, white pepper, boysenberry, toast, mocha, incense, graphite, mineral

Notes: Most of the wines in Argentina are comprised of 100 percent of the named grape, which is different from other countries, where you see more blends. Many of the wines are also grown at very high altitudes, with some vineyards as high as ten thousand feet above sea level.

Adventurous Chocolate Pairings

-  Conservative: Coffee Ganache Truffles
- Edgy: Dark chocolate infused with plum oil (available at TheChocolateTherapist.com)
- Gone Wild: Dark chocolate and cherry fudge

♇ MERITAGE ♇

Grapes used to make: Cabernet sauvignon, merlot, cabernet franc, Petit Verdot, Malbec, Carmenere, Gros Verdot. Meritage wines have a required 75 percent minimum blend of Bordeaux grape varietals.

Regions grown in: California/Napa Valley, Washington State, Chile

Body: Medium to full bodied with a long finish, can have smooth and soft tannins

Flavors: Dark berries, cherry, spice, coffee, dark cocoa, black olive, flowers, plum, toasty oak, berry cobbler, clove, vanilla, blackberry

Notes: The word *meritage* comes from a combination of the words *merit* and *heritage*, used to describe wines of merit with superior heritage. To use the term on the label, the release must be fewer than twenty-five thousand bottles and cannot be sold as a bargain-basement wine.

Adventurous Chocolate Pairings

- Conservative: Chocolate cherry cobbler
- Edgy: Thin piece of dark chocolate covered with chopped pistachios and optional melted Havarti cheese
- Gone Wild: Melt dark chocolate, stir in a sprinkle of ground clove and dried apricot bits, spread thin on wax paper, cool in refrigerator, break into bark.

MERLOT

Grapes used to make: Merlot, cabernet sauvignon

Regions grown in: France/Bordeaux, Italy, Australia, California/Napa Valley, Chile, Argentina, South Africa, New Zealand, Washington State, Long Island

Body: Medium bodied, soft tannins, supple texture, smooth, rich, easygoing flavor

Flavors: Oak, coffee, black cherry, blackberry, cassis, plum, violet, raisin, vegetable, dark chocolate, wild blueberry, vanilla, maple syrup, dried herbs, tea, milk chocolate, rose, jam

Notes: A broadly versatile wine, merlot spans the food charts in pairing. When venturing in chocolate, think spicy, fruity sauce, walnuts, subtly infused flavors, and even mint, for a few other possibilities outside the options below.

Adventurous Chocolate Pairings

- **Conservative: Chocolate poppy seed cake drizzled with dark chocolate**
- **Edgy: Dark chocolate peanut butter cup**
- **Gone Wild: Flourless chocolate torte with crumbled pistachios and raspberry sauce**

MOURVEDRE

Grapes used to make: Mourvedre, often blended with Grenache, Syrah, or other Rhone region grapes to improve its color and structure

Regions grown in: Italy, Australia/Barossa Valley, California/Napa Valley, Washington State, Spain, France

Body: Medium to full bodied, moderate to full tannins, high in alcohol

Flavors: Cedar, Asian spices, damp earth, game, plum, savory meats, smoke, ripe blackberry, raspberry, black cherry, apricot, chocolate, coffee, leather, oak, tar, toast, sweet wood, herbs

Notes: The savory elements of this grape lend it to unlimited pairings, especially savory chocolate dishes like chicken mole. Mourvedre's unique blend of earthy, gamey, and light red fruit flavors means you don't have to stop drinking just because dinner has ended—enjoy it with dessert too!

Adventurous Chocolate Pairings

- Conservative: Milk chocolate caramels
- Edgy: Dried mango dipped in a melted dark chocolate and ground ginger blend
- Gone Wild: Chocolate fondue with fresh berries and squares of pound cake for dipping

NEBBIOLO

Grapes used to make: Nebbiolo

Regions grown in: Italy/Piedmont, California/Napa Valley, Washington State, Argentina, Australia

Body: Medium to full bodied, silky tannins for a long, fresh finish, although it can be quite tannic when it's younger

Flavors: Rose, ripe fruit, spices, licorice, blackberry, oak, raspberry, cherry, glycerin, coffee, chocolate, smoke, tobacco, berry, plum, tar, herbs, prune

Notes: This late-harvest grape (October) forms the base some of Italy's most well-known wines, including Barolo and Barbaresco. It's typically a highly acidic grape, and wines made from the Nebbiolo pair best with the darker chocolates and intensely flavored infusions and inclusions.

Adventurous Chocolate Pairings

- Conservative: Pecan pie drizzled with dark chocolate

- 🌸 **Edgy: Melted dark chocolate with dried cherries and cinnamon**
- 🌸 **Gone Wild: Chocolate chip biscotti dipped in 60 percent or higher dark chocolate**

PETITE SIRAH

Grapes used to make: Petite Sirah, often blended with zinfandel to give density and structure. The grape is also called Durif.

Regions grown in: California/Napa Valley, Australia, France, Israel

Body: Full bodied, full tannins, smooth, lasting finish, high acidity, deeply colored

Flavors: Boysenberry, plum, blackberry, black pepper, ink, ripe fruits, jam, toasty oak, pomegranate, vanilla, dark chocolate, spice, anise, mocha, smoke

Notes: Like the bold Nebbiolo, this energetic wine is best paired with hearty chocolates and rich, flavorful infusions and inclusions. Its high acidity might be a challenge with chocolate, so you may have to work your way through a few different chocolates before finding the perfect pairing.

Adventurous Chocolate Pairings

- 🌸 **Conservative: Red velvet cake with melted milk chocolate**
- 🌸 **Edgy: Fresh berry tart with melted dark chocolate**
- 🌸 **Gone Wild: Melted dark chocolate and melted provolone cheese over a thinly toasted bagel**

PINOT NOIR

Grapes used to make Pinot noir

Regions grown in: France/Beaujolais and Burgundy, California, Oregon/Willamette Valley, Australia, South Africa, Germany, Switzerland, New Zealand, Italy

Body: Young, light to medium bodied, mild to moderate tannin, prominent acidity

Flavors: Cherry, raspberry, earth, leather, vanilla, jam, plum, licorice, cedar, mushrooms, strawberry, chocolate, mixed berries, smoke, violet, Asian spices, oak

Notes: A good pinot noir works with practically everything, from potato chips to roasted chicken and mushroom risotto. But take note when adding chocolate: give the wine a chance by looking for a medium-bodied, rather than a light-bodied wine so you still have a hope of tasting the wine once you've enjoyed your chocolate.

Adventurous Chocolate Pairings

- **Conservative: Chocolate cherry truffles**
- **Edgy: Flourless chocolate torte drizzled with raspberry purée and sprinkled with finely chopped almonds**
- **Gone Wild: A piece of 50 percent dark chocolate on a rice cracker topped with melted Swiss cheese (a great cheese with pinot noir)**

PORT, RUBY

Grapes used to make: Over one hundred grapes can be used in port, but the primary five are Tinta Barroca, Tinta Cao, Tempranillo, Touriga Francesa, and Touriga Nacional

Regions grown in: Portugal/Douro, Canada, Australia, India, Argentina, South Africa, United States

Body: Full bodied, fortified (clear brandy is added to port), beautiful deep red colors

Flavors: Dark fruit, red berries, strawberry, raspberry, cherry

Notes: The easiest way to remember which port pairs best with which chocolate is to think about color. Ruby port pairs well with chocolate with ruby or red-colored fruits like cherries, raspberries, cranberries, strawberries, and pomegranate. Tawny port (see the next category) works well with tan-colored inclusions such as nuts, spices, caramel, and toffee.

Adventurous Chocolate Pairings

- Conservative: Milk chocolate-covered caramels, optional sea salt
- Edgy: Dried, unsweetened mango dipped in melted dark chocolate with cinnamon oil
- Gone Wild: Milk chocolate cinnamon pecans (available at www.TheChocolateTherapist.com)

PORT, TAWNY

Grapes used to make: Over one hundred grapes can be used in port, but the primary five are Tinta Barroca, Tinta Cao, Tempranillo, Touriga Francesa, and Touriga Nacional.

Regions grown in: Portugal/Douro, Canada, Australia, India, Argentina, South Africa, United States

Body: Full bodied, fortified (clear brandy has been added)

Flavors: Nuts, pepper, fruit, caramel, toffee, black currant, maple syrup, apricot, orange, date, smoke, spice, cream, apricot

Notes: Tawny port is more delicate and flavorful than ruby port. Just as with ruby port, the easiest way to remember what pairs well with it is to think about color. Tawny ports are tanner in color, so they work best with chocolates that have tan-colored inclusions like spices, caramel, toffee, and nuts. Cinnamon is particularly good with tawny port. I highly recommend creating a few of your own cinnamon-infused adventures.

Adventurous Chocolate Pairings

- Conservative: Milk-chocolate-covered almond toffee with sea salt (www.TheChocolateTherapist.com)
- Edgy: Dark chocolate cashew turtles

🍇 **Gone Wilde: Candied orange peel dipped in lightly blended dark and milk chocolate**

RIOJA

Grapes used to make: Tempranillo, Garnacha Tinta, Mazuelo, Graciano. True Riojas are composed of primarily Tempranillo (60 percent), and Garnacha (20 percent), with the other varietals making up the difference.

Regions grown in: Northern Spain

Body: Medium to full bodied, elegant, soft, high alcohol, full and ripe tannins

Flavors: Fruits, strawberry, oak, vanilla, plum, dark chocolate, cherry, berry, nut, earth, graphite, espresso roast, black currant

Notes: The popular Rioja Gran Reserva wine spends at least two years in an oak barrel and three years in the bottle. Oak and vanilla are the featured flavors, making a vanilla-infused chocolate dessert the perfect partner in pairing.

Adventurous Chocolate Pairings

- 🍇 **Conservative: Dark chocolate mousse with cream and vanilla**
- 🍇 **Edgy: Chocolate cake with Chocolate Whipped Cream***
- 🍇 **Gone Wild: Melt 75 percent dark chocolate, stir in chopped almonds, macadamia nuts, and dried cherries, spread thin on wax paper, cool in refrigerator, and break into bark**

SANGIOVESE

Grapes used to make: Sangiovese, (when cabernet sauvignon, merlot, and Syrah are added, these varietals make up the Super Tuscan wines)

Regions grown in: Italy/Tuscany, California, Argentina, Romania, France, Australia

Body: Light to medium bodied, moderate to high acidity

Flavors: Earth, herbs, black cherry, strawberry, blueberry, flowers, plum, violet, orange, clove, cinnamon, thyme

Notes: As Professional Friends of Wine puts it on its site, "Sangiovese is to Chianti as Cabernet Sauvignon is to Bordeaux." These grapes form the base of the respective wines, although they are enjoyable on their own as well. When pairing with chocolate, focus on dark chocolates with a lower percentage of cocoa so you don't overpower the wine.

Adventurous Chocolate Pairings

- **Conservative: Milk chocolate maple**
- **Edgy: Double chocolate brownies with sliced strawberries**
- Gone Wild: Dark chocolate infused with Earl Grey (available at www.TheChocolateTherapist.com, Wine Pairing Chocolates)

SHIRAZ/SYRAH

Grapes used to make: Shiraz also called Syrah, Viognier, Grenache, Mourvedre, cabernet sauvignon. Shiraz is almost always blended with other grapes.

Regions grown in: Australia, California, South Africa, France/Rhone Valley. The name Shiraz is primarily used for wines from Australia, South Africa, Argentina, Chile, and Canada, while France and the United States use Syrah. It's the same grape masquerading under separate names.

Body: Full bodied, generally powerful, robust, long lived, tannic

Flavors: Spice, black pepper, tar, black fruit, plum, blackberry, raspberry, licorice, dark chocolate, bitter mocha, flowers, cream, rubber, black currant, salt, molasses, caramel, toast, blueberry, vanilla, acacia, earth, wood, cola, lychee, blackberry liqueur, cassis, mineral, white chocolate, cinnamon

Notes: A quick preview of the many flavors in Shiraz and it's hard to imagine a chocolate that *doesn't* pair with it. A typically spicy grape, it works nicely with spice-infused chocolates and especially well with eclectic truffles.

Adventurous Chocolate Pairings

- Conservative: Fruit and nut dark chocolate fondue
- Edgy: Dark cayenne pepper savouries
- Gone Wild: Dark chocolate caramels topped with chili pepper powder

TEMPRANILLO

Grapes used to make: This black grape is generally used to make European table wines and port. It's rarely produced as its own wine and, depending on the type of wine being made, will be blended with Grenache, Carignan, Graciano, merlot, and/or cabernet sauvignon.

Regions grown in: Spain, Argentina, South Africa, California/Napa Valley, Australia, Canada

Body: Medium to full bodied, soft, long on finish, low sugar, higher acidity when younger

Flavors: Violet, blackberry, raspberry, truffles, smoke, spice, tobacco, leather, herbs, plum, cherry, strawberry, vanilla, oak, chocolate

Notes: Like many reds, chocolate and berries are usually a good bet when pairing. Treat it like other full-bodied reds by edging your chocolate toward the darker side.

Adventurous Chocolate Pairings

- Conservative: Dark chocolate mint brownies (add one-half teaspoon of mint to your favorite recipe)
- Edgy: Hazelnut biscotti dipped in milk or dark chocolate
- Gone Wild: Dark chocolate and Havarti cheese on thin crackers

♟ VALPOLICELLA ♟

Grapes used to make: Corvina Veronese, Rondinella, Molinara

Regions grown in: Italy/Veneto and Valpolicella

Body: Light to medium body, full flavor, long finish, fragrant

Flavors: Cherry, raspberry, strawberry, jam, milk chocolate, licorice, smoke, wood, spice, oak, black fruit

Notes: Valpolicella is one of Italy's most produced wines, some say second only to Chianti. Its full fruit flavors and aromas make it easy to pair with chocolate, although consider the lower percentage dark chocolates as opposed to 70 percent and higher.

Adventurous Chocolate Pairings

- Conservative: **Dark chocolate raspberry** (available at www.TheChocolateTherapist.com, Wine Pairing Chocolates)
- **Edgy: Dark or milk chocolate cinnamon truffles**
- **Gone Wild: Almond and coconut chocolate chip tart with chocolate merlot sauce**

♟ ZINFANDEL ♟

Grapes used to make: Zinfandel, Petite Sirah

Regions grown in: California, Croatia, South Africa, Australia

Body: Generally full bodied, but can also be medium, usually tannic, rich, big flavor

Flavors: Spice, smoke, berry, raspberry, blackberry, anise, black cherry, nuts, chocolate, pepper, jam, cinnamon, ginger

Notes: Zinfandel grapes produce a considerably high-alcohol wine, occasionally approaching the 15 percent alcohol mark. Concerned imbibers will do well with chocolate and nuts, which will help slow absorption of the alcohol into the bloodstream. Spices also work wonderfully with this powerful, peppery provision.

Adventurous Chocolate Pairings

- 🍫 Conservative: Dark chocolate chai (available at www.TheChocolateTherapist.com, Pairing Chocolates)
- 🍫 Edgy: Dark chocolate with chili pepper
- 🍫 Gone Wild: Dark chocolate brownies with raspberry sauce

6 White Wine and Chocolate Pairings

When I first started teaching chocolate and wine pairing classes, I rarely used white wines. As time passed, I started venturing into predictable whites such as Moscato d'Asti, Riesling, and even chardonnay. But when we teach the classes now, we're on the "everything is worth a try" plan. In fact, for this book, I tossed all preconceived ideas aside to create a full collection of pairing possibilities for the adventurer. Since there are no precise rules in chocolate and wine pairing due to the wide variety of palates, personal discovery is easily the best measure of success.

White wines are often associated with white grapes, but the fact is that white wines occasionally include red or even black grapes. The skins are removed prior to fermentation to keep the wine white.

The sweetness of the wine depends on the length of time it's fermented, as well as how long the grapes are left on the vine. Wines start out fairly sweet, and as they're allowed to age, the grape's natural sugars are converted into alcohol. Longer processing equates to less sugar, more alcohol, and a drier wine.

More than 90 percent of the world's white wines come from three grapes: Riesling, sauvignon blanc, and chardonnay. Riesling is considered the sweetest and one of the easiest to pair with chocolate or a chocolate-based dessert. Sauvignon blanc and chardonnay follow, both of which offer their own significant pairing adventures.

Other white grapes include chenin blanc, Viognier, Semillon, pinot grigio, pinot blanc, pinot gris, Albarino, and gewürztraminer, but this is far from the entire list. White wine enthusiasts will be thrilled to learn that there are more than fifty major white grapes varieties to explore.

As with the red wine discussion, you won't necessarily taste every flavor listed in the wine descriptions, but they're included to help you identify various possibilities. Refer to the "Wine Aroma Wheel" for more ideas. And just like the red wine section, all recipes with an asterisk (*) can be found in the back of this book.

CHABLIS

Grapes used to make: Chardonnay

Regions grown in: France/Chablis and Burgundy

Body: Medium to full bodied, long finish, dry

Flavors: Lemon, fig, flowers, steel, mineral, slate, green apple, earth

Notes: Chablis is produced from 100 percent white grapes, unlike many white wines, which contain a percentage of red grapes as well. Chablis normally pairs well with cream-based savory dishes, so consider adding a little cream to your chocolate when pairing as well. Because the wine is typically served chilled, let the chocolate dessert sit in your mouth for just a few seconds to begin to melt before you sip the wine.

Adventurous Chocolate Pairings

- **Conservative: Chocolate Key Lime Pie with melted 60 percent dark chocolate**
- **Edgy: Fresh orange wedges dipped in melted dark chocolate and sprinkled with white chocolate shavings**

- Gone Wild: Green apples dipped in caramel sauce and milk chocolate

CHAMPAGNE

Grapes used to make: Chardonnay, pinot noir, pinot meunier

Regions grown in: France/Champagne (the only authentic Champagne), Italy

Body: Dry (brut), semidry (extra dry), semisweet (sec), sweet (demi-sec); white grapes make lighter Champagnes; red grapes make fuller Champagnes

Flavors: Grapefruit, lemon, citrus, apple, yeast, toast, mineral

Notes: Brut and extra dry are better served before and during dinner, while sec and demi-sec work better with chocolate and desserts. Finer Champagnes have smaller bubbles and more of them: look in the narrow part of the Champagne glass to see them best.

Adventurous Chocolate Pairings

- Conservative: Fresh strawberries dipped in white chocolate, a Champagne classic
- Edgy: Apple pie with melted milk chocolate and coconut flakes
- Gone Wild: White chocolate rose truffles (available at www.VosgesChocolates.com)

CHARDONNAY

Grapes used to make: Chardonnay

Regions grown in: France/Burgundy, California, Australia, Chile, New Zealand, Long Island, Washington State

Body: Medium to full bodied, dry, creamy texture

Flavors: Tart apple, citrus, lemon, pear, melon, toast, pineapple, vanilla, nuts, butter, wild mushrooms, peach, oak, herb, pineapple, kiwi, smoke, lime zest, jasmine, freesia, honeydew, mineral, earth, hazelnut

Notes: Chardonnay is generally aged in oak barrels and has a rich, buttery flavor. This makes it an obvious choice for luscious apple pie and chocolate, among other chocolate delights. After years of pairing adventures, we discovered it also seems to have a particular affinity to milk chocolate and all types of orange fruits.

Adventurous Chocolate Pairings

- **Conservative: Milk chocolate infused with organic oil (www.TheChocolateTherapist.com)**
- **Edgy: Dark chocolate with chili pepper**
- **Gone Wild: Thinly sliced bagel with goat cheese, cocoa nibs, and honey (idea courtesy of Prairie Berry Winery)**

CHENIN BLANC

Grapes used to make: Chenin blanc

Regions grown in: California, France/Loire Valley, South Africa, Australia

Body: Light to medium body, crisp, high acidity; very dry to very sweet depending on the region where it's grown; occasionally made as dessert wine

Flavors: Apple pie, pear, tart green apple, honey, nuts, wax, damp straw, honeycomb, pepper, grapes, apricot, fruit flowers, mineral, melon, lime, nectarine, peach, quince, clove, cream

Notes: Chenin blanc offers up a bit of a challenge for chocolate pairing with its high acidity, so be prepared for a true pairing adventure!

Adventurous Chocolate Pairings

- **Conservative: Berry pie drizzled with melted milk chocolate and sprinkled with cinnamon**

- Edgy: Dried peaches dipped in milk chocolate
- Gone Wild: Milk chocolate and Camembert cheese on a rice cake

 GEWÜRZTRAMINER

Grapes used to make: Gewürztraminer

Regions grown in: France/Alsace, California, Germany, Northern Italy, Washington State, Austria

Body: Medium bodied, lower acidity, low-alcohol; ranges from dry to sweet, depending on where the grapes are grown and the time they're harvested

Flavors: Allspice, clove, flowers, cinnamon, ginger, white pepper, rose water, lychee, citrus, honeysuckle, pink grapefruit, green apple, melon, apricot, peach, mint, licorice, roasted almond, fruit

Notes: Depending on how it's produced, this highly fruit-flavored wine is often quite sweet. Look for late-harvest Gerwürztraminer for added sweetness. As such, it lends itself nicely to a variety of chocolate pairings. Keep fruit in the picture, and you can hardly go wrong.

Adventurous Chocolate Pairings

- Conservative: Milk- or dark-chocolate-covered candied orange peel
- Edgy: Ginger cookies dipped in melted milk chocolate
- Gone Wild: Milk chocolate infused with organic apricot oil (available at www.TheChocolateTherapist.com, Pairing Chocolates)

 MUSCAT/MOSCATO

Grapes used to make: Muscat (considered the oldest varietal of all grapes)

Regions grown in: France/Loire Valley, Greece, Italy/Piedmont, Australia, California, Chile

Body: Light, sweet, low-alcohol, a bit bubbly: from Asti, expect a sparkling Italian wine, while wines from Alsace tend to be drier. Head to southern France for sweet dessert wines.

Flavors: Peach, apricot, orange, honey, spice, berry, tangerine, lemon, grape, musk, pear, white flowers; flavors vary depending on the region: Alsace and Samos have more tangerine; wines from Asti have more honey and floral notes.

Notes: This very sweet, low-alcohol dessert wine pairs wonderfully with orange fruits: oranges, apricots, peaches, mangos, papayas. Milk or dark chocolate, or both—why not?

Adventurous Chocolate Pairings

- Conservative: Milk chocolate infused with Amaretto oil (available at www.TheChocolateTherapist.com, Wine Pairing Chocolates)
- Edgy: Fresh orange and peach fruits slices with Chocolate Whipped Cream*
- Gone Wild: Dark chocolate infused with organic lemon oil (available at www.TheChocolateTherapist.com, Wine Pairing Chocolates)

PINOT BLANC

Grapes used to make: Pinot blanc

Regions grown in: Oregon, California, Italy/Alto Adige, France/Alsace

Body: Light to medium bodied, high acid, low sugar, clean, dry, crisp, long finish

Flavors: Melon, peach, nectar, honey, mineral, lime zest, nectarine, vanilla, wet stones, cider, chalk, lemon zest, walnut, green apple, spice

Notes: This clean, crisp wine makes a nice opening cocktail, guaranteed to wake up your guests and bring everyone into the moment. Once everyone has arrived, make sure they stay focused with an array of spicy, fruit-chocolate options.

Adventurous Chocolate Pairings

- Conservative: Apricot oat bars drizzled with milk chocolate
- Edgy: Thinly sliced red apples topped with honey, melted dark chocolate and a sprinkle of cinnamon
- Gone Wild: Muenster cheese, walnuts, and honey mixed together, served on top of a piece of dark chocolate

PINOT GRIGIO/GRIS

Grapes used to make: Pinot grigio or pinot gris

Regions grown in: France/Alsace, Italy, California, Oregon, New Zealand, Austria

Body: Full bodied, sometimes dry and spicy, sometimes sweet

Flavors: Spice, honey, nuts, fruit, smoke, pastry

Notes: Flavors vary considerably from region to region, but chances are good you'll be happy with high acidity fruits that match the acidity of the wine. Dare you go where no man has paired before?

Adventurous Chocolate Pairings

- Conservative: Dark chocolate with sliced almonds and a sprinkle of sea salt, try The Chocolate Therapist's "Down by the Sea Salt" bar at <u>www.TheChocolateTherapist.com</u>
- Edgy: Peach pie drizzled with melted milk chocolate
- Gone Wild: Chocolate biscotti dipped in melted dark chocolate sprinkled with cinnamon

🍷 RIESLING 🍷

Grapes used to make: Riesling

Regions grown in: Germany, Australia, France/Alsace, Washington State, New York, Austria, California/Sonoma, New Zealand, Italy, Canada, China, Italy

Body: Light bodied, crisp, sharp acidity, low alcohol: depending on the region, can be dry, semisweet, sweet, or sparkling

Flavors: Honey, flowers, apple, pear, peach, melon, mineral, petrol, kerosene, rubber, mango, guava, citrus, vanilla, apricot, orange, lime, slate, strawberry cream, lychee

Notes: Select a late-harvest Riesling when pairing with chocolate: you'll get a sweeter wine better suited to chocolate desserts.

Adventurous Chocolate Pairings

- **Conservative: Dried mango dipped in melted milk chocolate with optional sliced strawberries**
- **Edgy: Dark chocolate cake with Chocolate Whipped Cream and fresh orange slices**
- **Gone Wild: Thinly sliced dark chocolate, melted Brie cheese, and crushed filberts**

🍷 SAUVIGNON BLANC 🍷

Grapes used to make: Sauvignon Blanc, Semillon

Regions grown in: France, California, Australia, Chile, South Africa, Washington State, New Zealand

Body: Medium to full bodied, high acidity, crisp, clear, tangy: dryer wines come from Graves and Pessac-Leognan; sweeter options hail from Sauternes and Barsac

Flavors: Grapefruit, zest, gooseberry, asparagus, fruit salad, smoke, hay, fresh herbs, lime, citrus, mineral, lemon grass, plum, straw, gooseberry, passion fruit, kiwi, pear, cantaloupe, orange peel

Notes: Also known as Fumé Blanc, expect a grassy flavor and possibly some oak along with this wine's typically acidic fruit flavors. Definitely a long shot when pairing with chocolate, but guaranteed excitement for the *true* adventurer.

Adventurous Chocolate Pairings

- Conservative: Milk chocolate amaretto <u>(available at www.TheChocolateTherapist.com, Pairing Chocolates)</u>
- Edgy: Fresh pear dipped in melted milk chocolate infused with ground nutmeg
- Gone Wild: Chocolate cream pie sprinkled with chopped dried papaya and optional Chocolate Whipped Cream

SEMILLON

Grapes used to make: Semillon, sauvignon blanc, Muscadelle, chardonnay

Regions grown in: France/Bordeaux, Australia, California, Washington State, Chile

Body: Light to medium bodied, low acidity

Flavors: Lime, toast, cheese, peach, apricot, herb, honey, citrus, pineapple, vanilla

Notes: Semillon is more often blended with other grapes, rather than offered on its own. Dry wine enthusiasts will want to choose wines from the Sauternes region of Bordeaux. Those looking for something sweeter would do well with Australian and Washington wines.

Adventurous Chocolate Pairings

- Conservative: Dried peaches dipped in melted milk chocolate

- Edgy: Milk chocolate apricot (available at
  www.TheChocolateTherapist.com, Pairing Chocolates)
- Gone Wild: Thin rice crackers topped with melted Mozzarella
  cheese and dark chocolate shavings

SHERRY

Grapes used to make: Palomino, Pedro Ximenez

Regions grown in: Germany, Spain, Italy, France

Body: Dry (manzanilla or fino), dry to medium (amontillado or oloroso), sweet (cream)

Flavors: Nuts, caramel, hazelnut, walnut, fig, molasses, dates, smoke, green apple

Notes: Sherry is a fortified wine, meaning neutral brandy has been added to the wine to raise the alcohol content. With sherry, the brandy is added after fermentation. In port, it's added before. Cream sherry pairs wonderfully with chocolate, but don't hesitate to venture into a variety of Sherry options.

Adventurous Chocolate Pairings

- **Conservative:** Peanut butter cookies dipped in milk chocolate
- **Edgy:** Melted dark chocolate with cinnamon and chopped walnuts
- **Gone Wild:** Double Dark Chocolate Brownies* topped with honey and chopped almonds

VOUVRAY

Grapes used to make: Chenin blanc

Regions grown in: France

Body: Dry, semisweet or sweet

Flavors: Fruit, mineral, lemon, apple, pear, peach, flowers

Notes: Now is as good a time as any to pull out this much-loved cliché: "Like a box of chocolates, you just never know what you're going to get," unless, of course, you know your Vouvray. The wine varies greatly from region to region, like many of the white wines. Sweeter is better with chocolates, of course.

Adventurous Chocolate Pairings

- Conservative: **Peach cobbler with chocolate sauce**
- Edgy: **Red apple slices with melted Monterey Jack cheese and topped with semisweet dark chocolate chips.**
- Gone Wild: **Lemon meringue pie drizzled with melted dark chocolate**

WHITE ZINFANDEL

Grapes used to make: Zinfandel

Regions grown in: California

Body: Light, soft, low in alcohol, sweet, tangy

Flavors: Vanilla, cherry, orange, raspberry, lime, plum, strawberry, pineapple, pear

Notes: White zinfandel is made from red zinfandel grapes that have had the skins peeled off before fermentation. The resulting wine is very light, generally quite sweet, and often snubbed by true wine enthusiasts. Fabulous! This means more for those who appreciate a relaxed, fresh wine that offers a collection of interesting chocolate pairings.

Adventurous Chocolate Pairings

- Conservative: **Dried cherries and coconut flakes swirled into melted milk chocolate**

- **Edgy:** Strawberry shortcakes drizzled with milk or dark chocolate
- **Gone Wild:** Vanilla wafers and milk chocolate, topped with sliced pears

Appendix A: Quick Reference Guide

Moscato	Pinot Noir	Zinfandel	Cabernet
Peach	Blueberry	Cinnamon	Cherry
Mango	Cashew	Pecan	Raspberry
Apricot	Milk chocolate	Nutmeg	Almond
Orange	Blackberry	Chili pepper	Blackberry
Nectarine	Hemp seed	Strawberry	Mint

Wine Shopping Strategy

You can either pair the wine with the chocolate or the chocolate with the wine. I generally start with the chocolate and pair it with the wine because I like chocolate more than wine. For me, having the perfect chocolate outweighs the importance of the wine. Many people, however, prefer to choose the wine first and pair the chocolate with the wine.

Smaller specialty shops generally offer wines that the owners or buyers have tasted and hand-selected. For diversity, look for stores with a nice international selection that includes wines from Argentina, Chile, South Africa, New Zealand, and Australia.

If you already have your chocolate or dessert idea in mind, look for wines that list similar flavors to what you're serving. Many wines have entertaining and informative descriptions on the labels, but if not, this is where the store owner or information cards above the wines (in some stores) will come in handy.

Appendix B: Chocolate and Wine Pairing Basics: A Summary

1. Taste both the chocolate and the wine in the same order as if you were at an individual chocolate-tasting or wine-tasting event. Sample lighter wines and chocolates first, and move to heavier flavors from there.

2. Cleanse the palate with salt-free crackers or pretzels and drink a room-temperature water between pairings.

3. It's best to limit the pairings to six wines and chocolates in a single event. Any more than that and taste buds may become desensitized, losing their ability to differentiate flavors.

4. Typically, light wines work better with a lighter chocolate, while the heavier, more-robust wines are better with darker chocolates. A heavy wine can overpower the chocolate, and vice versa.

5. Fortified wines (such as port and sherry) pair exceptionally well with chocolate because they're sweet and bold, making it possible for pairing success with a wider variety of chocolates.

6. Wines with similar attributes as the chocolate work well together. For example, a fruity wine will better serve a chocolate with fruit nuances. This is called synergy: the two ideally match each other in some way and enhance the flavors of both.

7. A sweeter chocolate, like milk or white chocolate, can make some wines taste bitter and astringent. Again, work to match the sweetness of the wine to the sweetness of the chocolate.

8. Bittersweet chocolates generally go best with stronger red wines, especially wines that have a slightly roasted and bitter flavor with their own chocolate notes.

9. Milk and white chocolates pair well with dessert wines such as Moscato, port, and very-sweet white wines.

10. Tannic wines work better with rich, heavy chocolates with extra cocoa butter or cream. The butter in the chocolate helps mellow the tannic element of the wine, although the chocolate can still make the wine bite.

11. For easy success with ports, pair them by their colors: Ruby port pairs well with ruby-colored infusions like berries, cherries, and strawberries. Tawny port generally works quite well with tan-colored infusions such as nuts, caramel, spices, and toffees.

Great Wine Websites

Bon Appétit magazine	www.epicurious.com
Decanter magazine	www.decanter.com
Easy French Food	www.EasyFrenchFood.com
Food & Wine magazine	www.FoodandWine.com
Gourmet Sleuth	www.GourmetSleuth.com
Happy Hour Alert	www.HappyHourAlert.com
My Wines Direct	www.MyWinesDirect.com
Professional Friends of Wine	www.WinePros.org
Wine Club Central	www.WineClubCentral.com
Wine Enthusiast Magazine	www.WineMag.com
Wine Intro	www.WineIntro.com
Winemaking	www.WineMaking.com
Wine Spectator magazine	www.WineSpectator.com
Wine.com	www.Wine.com

Appendix C: How to Microwave Chocolate

Many of the suggested wine and chocolate pairings call for you to make your own concoctions of melted chocolate with nuts, berries, spices, and naturally-flavored oils. This section will have you creating your own extraordinary recipes in no time. In just one to three minutes, your chocolate creation will be ready to go.

Chocolate is a bit finicky. When melted improperly, your delightful creation can turn into a scorched, "seized" chocolate mass. Fortunately, once you learn the technique, it's almost fail proof.

The main caveats in microwaving chocolate are: do it slowly and use low heat. It also works best when done in a glass bowl (not ceramic or plastic). Make sure there's absolutely no water in the bowl, or your chocolate may seize up into an ugly chunk.

1. Pour the chocolate pieces into the bowl, up to about half full.
2. Reduce the microwave heat by 50 percent.
3. Microwave for thirty seconds, remove the bowl, and stir the chocolate (not much has happened yet).
4. Reduce microwave heat by 50 percent again.
5. Microwave again for thirty seconds, remove, and stir.
6. Let the chocolate begin to melt on its own.
7. Reduce heat to 50 percent, microwave, and stir again.
8. Repeat as needed, always remembering to reduce the heat by 50 percent each time you put the bowl back into the microwave.

Remove the chocolate just before it is completely melted and stir the remaining chunks until they melt. Melted chocolate is best for dipping, mixing, and serving immediately. It won't naturally harden into the same form it was in before you started unless you've tempered it, that is, heated it and then cooled it to the exact temperature required to reset the original form. If you want to dip chocolates that you plan to serve later, you'll need to refrigerate them to harden them.

Tempering is done to get chocolate to re-form beautifully once you've dipped or made whatever you're going to create. It's best done with a tempering machine. I've tried doing it in the microwave and on the stove with a candy thermometer, and it works great if you happen to have an extra ten days to experiment. Short of that, use the refrigerator or buy a tempering machine.

Appendix D: Recipes

Chocolate Kahlua Truffles (Kristin Renzema)

12 ounces semisweet dark organic chocolate chips
½ cup heavy cream (*not* half-and-half)
½ stick butter (do not use margarine)
1 tablespoon instant coffee granules
2 tablespoons Kahlua
¼ tsp of salt
Cocoa powder for dusting

Combine all ingredients except the cocoa powder in a small saucepan. Heat over low heat, stirring occasionally until very smooth. Chill the mixture in a covered container, in the refrigerator until it's firm (approximately one hour). Take heaping tablespoons of the mixture, form them into one-inch balls, and roll each ball in the cocoa powder. Store the truffles in the refrigerator or the freezer for up to one month.

Chocolate Key Lime Pie

This is a speed baker's no-bake version.
1 can (14 ounces) of sweetened condensed milk
Juice from 4 limes
Juice from 2 lemons
1½ cups heavy whipping cream (or use 16 ounces Cool Whip)
¼ cup baking cocoa powder
4 tablespoons pure cane sugar or agave nectar
1 prepared graham cracker crust

In a small bowl, mix the milk with the juice of the lemons and limes and set aside. In a medium-sized bowl, mix the heavy cream with a mixer until it forms stiff peaks. Stir in cocoa powder and sugar, then add the juice-milk mixture. Stir until just mixed. Pour into prepared crust, and let refrigerate for at least one hour before serving.

Chocolate Whipped Cream

½ cup heavy cream
1 tablespoon cocoa powder
1 tablespoon pure cane sugar
Grated dark chocolate (optional)

In a medium bowl, whip cream with a mixer until it forms stiff peaks. Add cocoa powder and sugar (adjust amounts to personal taste) and blend in. To really impress guests, sprinkle some grated dark chocolate on top of the whipped cream.

Dark Chocolate Cake with Chocolate-Apricot Glaze

This is a speed baker's version, using a box of chocolate cake mix.
1 box chocolate cake mix, any brand
¼ cup baking cocoa powder

While preparing the cake according to the package directions, add the baking cocoa powder to the batter. Bake the cake according to box instructions and set aside to cool.

Chocolate-Apricot Glaze

1 cup pure apricot preserves (no sugar added)
½ cup orange juice
1 tablespoon agave nectar or honey
½ cup dark chocolate chips or chopped dark chocolate bar

In a small saucepan, combine preserves, orange juice, and agave nectar or honey and then stir over medium heat until melted. Reduce to low heat and stir in chocolate chips. Simmer uncovered on low heat for fifteen minutes or until mixture is thick enough to stay on the back of a spoon when dipped into the mixture. Drizzle or brush the glaze over the cake.

Dark Chocolate Vanilla Drizzle

8 ounces dark chocolate chips
1 teaspoon pure vanilla (do not use vanillin, an artificial flavoring)

Put the chocolate chips in a glass bowl. Microwave them on low heat, thirty seconds at a time, stirring each time until the chocolate is melted. Add the vanilla and stir. Drizzle onto pie, or anything else!

Double Dark Chocolate Brownies

This is a speed baker's rendition, using a boxed brownie mix.
1 box brownie mix, any brand
¼ cup baking cocoa
1 cup dark chocolate chips or 1 three-ounce dark chocolate bar, chopped

Preheat the oven to the temperature specified in the brownie mix directions. Follow the directions on the brownie box for mixing the batter. Add the cocoa and chocolate chips or chopped chocolate bar to the batter and bake the brownies according to the directions on the box.

Pomegranate & Cinnamon Dark Chocolate Brownies

Use the Double Dark Chocolate Brownies recipe, but when making the brownie mix, substitute pomegranate juice for the water in the recipe and add one teaspoon of cinnamon to the batter.

Gluten-Free Chocolate-Chip Oatmeal Cookies

½ cup shortening
¼ cup butter
¾ cup brown sugar
2 teaspoons pure vanilla extract
3 eggs
3 cups oat flour (make your own by grinding old-fashioned oats in the blender)
¼ cup dark organic cocoa powder
1 teaspoon baking soda
1 teaspoon salt
3 cup regular oats (not quick cooking)
2 3.5-ounce dark organic chocolate bars, chopped
¾ cup pecans, chopped (optional)

Preheat the oven to 350°F. In a large bowl, combine the shortening, butter, brown sugar, and vanilla and stir until blended. Add eggs and blend well. (Note: I prefer to stir cookie mix by hand because the cookies come out thicker and chewier than if you use an electric mixer, but feel free to choose either method.) Add the flour, cocoa powder, salt, and baking soda and mix well. Stir in the oats and mix well. Add the chopped chocolate and pecans (if using) and stir to distribute them throughout the mixture. Drop tablespoonfuls of the batter onto a lightly greased cookie sheet and bake for nine to ten minutes.

Haute Chocolate

To make this recipe lighter, substitute vanilla almond milk or rice milk, but note that the mixture will not get as thick as when you use half-and-half or whole milk. Also, you may want to try this without a sweetener, as the half-and-half makes the chocolate much sweeter.

4 ounces 65 percent or higher dark chocolate chips or chopped chocolate bar
2½ cups half-and-half or whole milk
3 tablespoons cocoa powder
½ teaspoon pure vanilla extract
2 tablespoons agave nectar or other sweetener (optional)
¼ teaspoon ancho or cayenne chili powder (optional)
Whipped cream and chopped nuts (optional)

Pour the half-and-half into a medium saucepan and turn the heat to medium, stirring constantly. Once hot, turn the heat to low, whisk in the chocolate and cocoa powder, and allow to simmer until the liquid has thickened slightly (make sure it doesn't boil). Add the vanilla, agave nectar, and ancho (if using), stir, then pour the liquid into four small coffee or tea cups. Garnish each cup with whipped cream and chopped nuts, if you prefer, and serve.

Raspberry/Pomegranate Purée

1 pound frozen raspberries, thawed and drained
½ cup pomegranate juice
2 tablespoons pomegranate juice
½ cup agave nectar, honey or raw cane sugar
1 tablespoon cornstarch

Combine the raspberries, half a cup of the pomegranate juice, and your sweetener of choice in a medium saucepan and bring to a boil; then allow it to simmer for fifteen minutes. Dissolve the cornstarch in the remaining two tablespoons of pomegranate juice and add this to the simmering mixture, stirring constantly. Continue to simmer until the purée is thickened. Spoon the purée over brownies, chocolate cake, chocolate pie, or the dessert of your choice.

Raspberry Truffle Brownies (Kristin Renzema)

¾ cup (1½ sticks) salted butter
4 ounces dark organic unsweetened chocolate, chopped
3 large eggs
2 cups sugar
⅓ cup raspberry jam
3 tablespoons black raspberry liqueur
1 cup all-purpose flour
¼ teaspoon salt
1 cup dark chocolate chips
Powdered sugar (optional)

Preheat the oven to 350°F. Spray a nine-inch-diameter springform pan with nonstick cooking spray. Melt the butter and chocolate in a large saucepan over low heat, stirring constantly until smooth. Remove from heat and set aside. Whisk in the eggs, sugar, jam, and liqueur. Stir in the flour and salt, then the chocolate chips. Transfer the batter to the prepared pan.

Bake the batter until a toothpick inserted in the center comes out with moist crumbs attached, about forty-five minutes. Let it cool in the pan on a rack for about an hour. When it has cooled completely, run a small knife around the edges of the pan to loosen it, then cut it into twelve squares. Dust the brownies with powdered sugar, if you prefer.

Tart Apple/Blackberry Pie

3 pounds thinly sliced green apples
1 pound fresh or frozen (thawed and drained) blackberries
¼ cup lemon juice
¾ cup pure cane sugar or raw sugar
½ cup flour (or ¾ cup oat flour for less gluten)
1 teaspoon cinnamon
½ teaspoon powdered cloves
Butter (softened)

Frozen pastry crust for single-crust pie, thawed and ready for baking

Preheat the oven to 375°F. In a large bowl, combine the apples, blackberries, and lemon juice and stir to coat the fruit with the lemon juice. In a small bowl, blend the sugar, flour, cinnamon, and cloves. Add the dry mixture to the apples and blackberries and toss until the fruit is well coated. Lightly butter the bottom of the piecrust. Pour the mixture into the piecrust and cover with foil. Bake the pie for thirty minutes. Remove the foil and bake for another thirty minutes, or until the apples are slightly soft (test lightly with a fork).

Dark Chocolate Truffles (Flavor variations below)

8 ounces whipping cream
½ cup (1 stick butter)
16 ounces 60 percent or higher dark chocolate, melted
Flavoring oils (see below)
Pure cocoa powder or cocoa powder and powdered sugar mixture

In a medium saucepan, heat the whipping cream over medium heat until it's boiling, stirring constantly. Remove from the heat, add the butter, and continue stirring until it's melted. Slowly add the butter and cream mixture to the melted chocolate. Add the various oils listed below, depending on the recipe.

Allow the truffle mixture to sit uncovered until it reaches room temperature, stirring occasionally. To speed up the process, the mixture can be put in the refrigerator until it reaches a consistency that can be rolled. Roll spoonfuls into half-inch balls, then roll each ball in pure cocoa powder, a cocoa powder and powdered sugar mixture, or various spices. The truffles can also be dipped in melted chocolate and refrigerated.

Add more flavors, if desired—the following recommendations are starting points. Note that if you have extra-strong flavoring oils, you may need less than these listed amounts. Start with small amounts and add a little at a time to flavor the truffles. The flavors listed here are oils, not flavorings or extracts. Oils are much stronger and are designed to flavor chocolates, so make sure you're using oils and not water-based extracts. You may purchase organic chocolate flavoring oils at www.NaturesFlavors.com.

Chili Pepper Truffles: ½ tablespoon chili oil

Coffee Ganache Truffles: ½ tablespoon coffee oil

Dark Chocolate Cherry Truffles: ½ tablespoon cherry oil

Raspberry Dark Chocolate Truffles: ½ tablespoon raspberry oil

Cinnamon Truffles: ½ teaspoon of cinnamon

References

Benjamin, Barbara Bloch. *The Little Black Book of Chocolate.* New York: Peter Pauper Press, 2003.

Coe, Sophie D., and Michael D. Coe. *The True History of Chocolate.* New York: Thames and Hudson, 1996.

Didio, Ton, and Amy Zovarto. *Renaissance Guide to Wine and Food Pairing.* Indianapolis, IN: Alpha Books, 2003.

Food and Wine Pairing.www.foodandwinepairing.org/food_pairing_board.html.

Jefford, Andrew. *Choosing Wine.* New York: Ryland Peter & Small, 2003.

Murdock, Linda. A Busy Cook's Guide to Spices: How to Introduce New Flavors to Everyday Meals. Denver, CO: Bellweather Book, 2007.

Murray, Michael T. *The Encyclopedia of Healing Foods.* New York: Atria Books, 2005.

The Pantry. Chocolate and Cocoa. Baking 911. Chocolate Basics. www.baking922.com/chocolate/basics.htm.

Pech, Julie. *The Chocolate Therapist: A User's Guide to the Extraordinary Health Benefits of Chocolate.* Hoboken, NJ: John Wiley and Sons, 2004.

Raffaldini. www.raffaldini.com/grapes.shtml.

Red Wine Academy. www.redwineacademy.com/types-of-redwine-grapes.html.

Ristoraunte Amarone. www.loscabosguide.com/amarone/index.html.

About the Author

Julie has embraced a passion for health and nutrition her entire life. A longtime competitor in sports, she was always interested in nutrition-for-performance. She studied nutrition and science in college and earned her degree in psychology from the University of Colorado in Denver.

Julie worked for Spyder Active Sports for twelve years before leaving to start her own company, then sold it five successful years later to follow her dream of becoming an author. Finally putting her passions together, she set out to prove that when you combine the mind, the body and chocolate, something extraordinary happens. A love for chocolate and a lifelong devotion to nutrition inspired Julie to writing her first book about chocolate: *The Chocolate Therapist: A User's Guide to the Extraordinary Health Benefits of Chocolate.*

Julie speaks regularly to groups of all kinds including corporations, women's groups, men's groups, luncheons, non-profits, for educational programs and more. She's developed her own line of all-natural chocolate, teaches chocolate and wine pairing classes and has traveled internationally as a guest lecturer on cruise ships educating people about chocolate.

Dare to Pair was originally presented in *The Chocolate Therapist* under the "Chocolate and Wine Pairing" chapter, but the popularity of chocolate and wine pairing private parties as well as the classes at Julie's shop inspired her to release a completely updated and larger version of the chapter as its own book. *Dare to Pair* includes all of her most up to date discoveries in chocolate and wine along with a significant amount of material that has not been printed previously.

To book a speaking engagement or private event, contact Julie at Julie@TheChocolateTherapist.com.   Other books by this author:

THE CHOCOLATE THERAPIST:

A USER'S GUIDE TO THE EXTRAORDINARY HEALTH BENEFITS OF CHOCOLATE

All the health benefits of chocolate condensed into a one-stop resource for chocolate lovers worldwide. This book is easy to read, entertaining and educational--a great gift for every occasion. Purchase here:

www.thechocolatetherapist.com

www.amazon.com (also available in kindle)

CHOCOLATE SOIREE:

HOW TO THROW THE ULTIMATE CHOCOLATE PARTY

Everything you've ever needed to know to host your own amazing chocolate party, including a 4-week planning guide, dozens of resources and referenced, along with free printable materials that can be used at any party.

www.thechocolatetherapist.com

A percentage of every sale on www.TheChocolateTherapist.com is donated to worldwide charity programs.